Frank N. Stine's Robot

Written by
Alan Durant

Illustrated by
Dynamo

Frank N. Stine was a shy boy. He found it hard to make friends. In fact, he had no friends at all and he always played on his own.

Frank loved making things. From empty cardboard boxes, plastic bottles, bubble wrap, broken coat hangers and other bits of junk, he built castles, football stadiums, racing cars, spaceships and time machines.

One day Frank's mum gave him a broken toaster – and that gave him an idea. He'd make himself a robot friend!

Frank took the toaster apart so that he could use the pieces and wires to make his robot. He found other things too: a broken hairdryer, an old kettle and a discarded computer keyboard …

On his way to and from school Frank looked in bins and on dumps for anything that might be useful.

When he found something, he always took it home and put it carefully with the other bits and pieces he had collected.

Frank's robot started to take shape. Frank made a head and a body, then arms and legs, feet and hands. He gave the robot a mouth and nose and eyes. He added more and more parts, making his robot bigger and better.

Day after day Frank tinkered happily with his robot. He talked to it as if it was really alive. The robot never talked back, of course, but Frank didn't mind that.

One stormy night, as the rain lashed against the skylight, Frank looked at his robot, lying still and silent on the floor, and he felt suddenly sad and lonely. The robot would never come to life and be a real, living friend, he thought gloomily, as he closed his eyes …

But something strange happened that night.

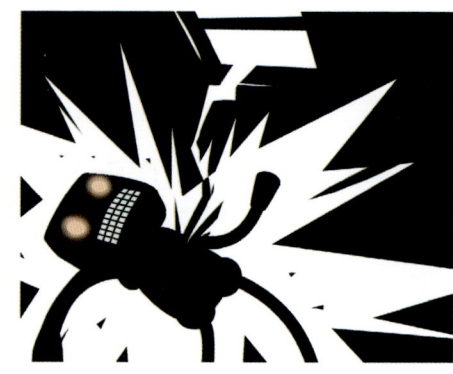

First, the wind rattled the skylight open. Then thunder rumbled and a bolt of lightning shot down through the sky, straight into Frank's room. The lightning struck the robot!

The robot twitched and jerked and jolted. Slowly – very slowly – it raised an arm, then another arm … a leg and another leg. Then it lifted its head.

When Frank woke in the morning, he was amazed to see his robot shuffling around the room. "You're alive!" he cried. "You're really alive!" He couldn't believe his eyes – and nor could his mum when the robot followed Frank down to breakfast.

The robot didn't seem to like toast or cereal, but he gobbled up the bag of nuts and bolts that Frank's mum found in the garage!

Frank couldn't wait to get back from school that afternoon. He rushed home and ran up to his room – and there was his robot, watching TV and munching an empty baked-bean can!

Frank showed the robot his toys and his models. He played games with him on the computer. He even read him stories. They had a great time together.

The days passed, but Frank never took his robot out of the house, because he wanted to keep the robot all to himself. He was Frank's special friend.

But the robot was curious. He saw the world outside through the window and he wanted to explore it.

So one night, when Frank was asleep, the robot crept outside …

The next morning, there was a rumpus in the village. There were stories of hubcaps missing from cars, knobs and knockers taken from front doors, street signs stolen.

"Mystery metal thief strikes in the night!" read the headline in the local paper.

The next night the same thing happened … and then the night after that …

Early one morning, there was a loud knock at the Stine's door. Mrs Stine opened it to find an angry crowd outside.

"We want the robot!" a man shouted.

"Bring him out!" cried another.

"Thief!" yelled a third.

Frank appeared with the robot behind him.

"What's wrong?" he asked.

One of the men told him that the robot had been seen stealing bits of metal. He'd been followed back to the Stine's house.

"He must be destroyed!" the crowd demanded.

"No!" cried Frank, but the crowd pushed forward and seized the robot. They dragged him away.

"Stop! Let him go!" It was the children on their way to school. They rushed excitedly to the robot and put their arms round him. They had never seen anything so wonderful.

The robot smiled and lifted them up into the air.

Frank explained that the robot had been hungry. He hadn't meant to steal. He didn't know that what he was doing was wrong.

Frank suggested a plan: the villagers could leave their unwanted scrap metal on the doorstep at night and the robot would collect and eat it. It would be good for everyone.

And so it was agreed.

From that time onwards, the robot never went hungry. He only took what was left for him and he never stole metal again. The children all loved him. He was a friend to them all.

As for Frank N. Stine, he was very happy to be sharing his robot with everyone. The robot had many, many friends, especially children, and every friend of the robot's was now also a friend of Frank's.

Best of all, Frank now had somebody whom he could call his best friend.

Can you guess who that was?